What are these animals doing?

Bobbie Kalman

Crabtree Publishing Company
www.crabtreebooks.com

Created by Bobbie Kalman

Dedicated by Crystal Sikkens
For Opa and Oma Egberts

Author and Editor-in-Chief
Bobbie Kalman

Editor
Kathy Middleton

Proofreader
Crystal Sikkens

Photo research
Bobbie Kalman
Crystal Sikkens

Design
Bobbie Kalman
Katherine Berti
Samantha Crabtree
(logo and front cover)

Production coordinator
Katherine Berti

Illustrations
Bonna Rouse: page 15

Photographs
© Dreamstime.com: pages 10, 11 (bottom), 23 (top left)
© iStockphoto.com: back cover, pages 11 (top), 22 (left)
© Photos.com: page 17 (top)
© Shutterstock.com: front cover, pages 1, 3, 4, 5, 7, 8, 9, 12, 13, 14, 15, 16, 17 (bottom), 18, 19, 20, 21, 22 (right), 23 (all except top left), 24 (all except camouflage)
Other images by Digital Vision

Library and Archives Canada Cataloguing in Publication

Kalman, Bobbie, 1947-
What are these animals doing? / Bobbie Kalman.

(Looking at nature)
Includes index.
ISBN 978-0-7787-3324-9 (bound).--ISBN 978-0-7787-3344-7 (pbk.)

1. Animal behavior--Juvenile literature. I. Title. II. Series: Kalman, Bobbie, 1947- . Looking at nature.

QL751.5.K347 2008 j591.5 C2008-907022-4

Library of Congress Cataloging-in-Publication Data

Kalman, Bobbie.
What are these animals doing? / Bobbie Kalman.
p. cm. -- (Looking at nature)
Includes index.
ISBN 978-0-7787-3344-7 (pbk. : alk. paper) -- ISBN 978-0-7787-3324-9 (reinforced library binding : alk. paper)
1. Animal behavior--Juvenile literature. I. Title. II. Series.

QL751.5.K337 2009
591.5--dc22

2008046270

Crabtree Publishing Company

www.crabtreebooks.com 1-800-387-7650

In Canada: We acknowledge the financial support of the Government of Canada through the Book Publishing Industry Development Program (BPIDP) for our publishing activities.

Published in Canada
Crabtree Publishing
616 Welland Ave.
St. Catharines, Ontario
L2M 5V6

Published in the United States
Crabtree Publishing
PMB16A
350 Fifth Ave., Suite 3308
New York, NY 10118

Published in the United Kingdom
Crabtree Publishing
White Cross Mills
High Town, Lancaster
LA1 4XS

Published in Australia
Crabtree Publishing
386 Mt. Alexander Rd.
Ascot Vale (Melbourne)
VIC 3032

Contents

What do animals do?

Some of the things that animals do may seem strange to us. Some animals change the way their bodies look. Some pretend to be other living things. Animals do the things they do to stay alive. This book shows pictures of animals. Guess what they are doing and why they **behave**, or act, the way they do. Have fun!

Why does this insect look like a tree branch? See page 7.

Why is this dog's tongue hanging out? See pages 20-21.

Why do chameleons change color? See pages 8-9.

Why is this bird dancing? See page 12.

How do they hide?

This gecko is hiding from **predators**. Predators are animals that eat other animals. Why is it hard to see the gecko? The gecko is the same color as the tree bark under it. It is **camouflaged**, or hidden.

*This gecko's **texture** also looks rough, like the texture of tree bark. Texture is how something looks and feels.*

Camouflage helps some animals blend in with their homes. Camouflage is having colors, shapes, or textures that help animals hide. Some insects do not look like insects. They look like parts of plants.

This katydid looks more like a leaf than an insect!

Instead of an insect, this unicorn mantis looks just like a branch with a leaf growing on it. It is using ***mimicry****. Mimicry is pretending to be something else.*

What colors are they?

Chameleons are lizards. What happens to the skin colors of chameleons? Why does it happen?

Chameleons change their colors. They do not do it for camouflage. Their colors change as their moods change. Their colors also change when the light or heat around them changes. Chameleons can change only the colors that are in their skin. What colors does this chameleon have in its skin?

colors in skin

Why do they do that?

This male anole has puffed out the skin under its jaw. This skin is called a **dewlap**. Why does the anole do that? Why do porcupine fish sometimes make their bodies bigger?

The dewlap makes the anole look bigger to predators. It also tells other male anoles to stay away!

dewlap

Porcupine fish have **spines** on their bodies. Spines are like sharp needles. When a porcupine fish sees a predator, it swallows water and makes itself bigger. Its spines stick out. A predator will not try to eat a big fish with sharp spines!

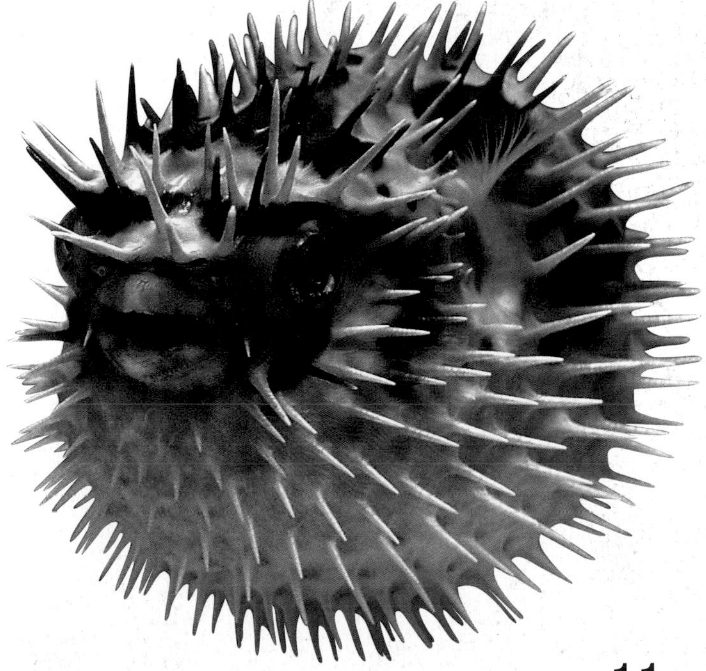

Sing and dance

Some male animals sing and dance. Why do they do it? They do it to find **mates**, or partners. The males and females will then become parents together.

This male blue-footed booby is dancing for a female. Will he win her heart?

Male humpback whales look like they are dancing when they leap high out of the water. They do it to find mates. These whales also sing beautiful songs under water. The songs are up to an hour long!

Where do they go?

Some animals leave home and then come back again. Many birds fly away for the cold winter months. Some animals move to places where there is more water and food. Moving from one place to another is called **migration**.

More than a million wildebeest cross this river each year. They migrate to other areas where there are plenty of new grasses to eat.

Many birds fly to warmer places for winter, where they can find food to eat. These sandhill cranes are migrating birds. They will fly home again in the spring when it is warm, and there is plenty of food.

egg

Sea turtles swim back to the beaches where they **hatched** from eggs. They swim a very long way! They lay their eggs on the same beaches.

hatching turtle

Caring for their babies

A **mammal** is an animal with some hair or fur on its body. How do mammal mothers look after their babies? Mammal mothers can feed their babies milk from their bodies. This seal pup was just born. Its mother is feeding it milk from her body. Drinking mother's milk is called **nursing**.

Why is this cougar mother carrying her **cub**, or baby, like that? Carrying the cub by the **scruff**, or back of the neck, is the easiest way to move it. It does not hurt the cub and keeps it quiet. Mammal mothers move their babies often to keep them safe.

This bear mother is teaching her cub how to fish for salmon. Bear cubs stay with their mothers for over four years. Their mothers teach them how to stay alive.

True or false?

Oh, my! Is it true or a lie? Is this bug dead? No, the weevil is only playing dead to fool predators that hunt living animals. Playing dead is how a weevil stays alive!

Oh, my!

Are these dolphins smiling? Are they telling jokes? Why are there small fish and shrimp on the moray eel's head? Will the moray eel eat these animals?

Dolphins always look like they are smiling, but they do not tell jokes.

The moray eel will not eat these small animals. They are cleaning its skin. Cleaners eat the dead skin and smaller animals that are on the eel's skin.

Tongue teasers

Why do animals stick out their tongues? Are they angry? Are they making fun? Guess why these animals are showing their tongues. Do not read the answers until you have made your guesses!

Why are these dogs' tongues hanging loose?

Why does a snake stick out its tongue?

Answers:

1. Dogs **pant** to cool off. To pant is to breathe quickly. It is like **sweating**. Dogs sweat, or lose water, through their tongues.
2. Snakes use their tongues to find out if there is food nearby.
3. Cats use their tongues to clean their fur.
4. A giraffe's tongue can be 18 inches (46 cm) long! Giraffes eat the leaves of acacia trees, which have thorns. They use their long tongues to reach around the thorns. Their tongues are blue to keep from getting sunburned.
5. Chameleons use their long sticky tongues to catch insects.

Why is the kitten licking its fur?

Why are giraffe tongues long and blue?

Say this five times! Sticky tongues snag slippery insects!

What do you think?

Write a funny poem or story about what you think the animals are doing in each picture. The questions can get you started, or you may have some better ideas!

Am I a winner?

Would you like to dance?

Can I please go and play?

Do you want to be friends?

What tastes so yucky?

How do you like my shorts?

Words to know and Index

Printed in the U.S.A. - BG